M000220814

The Emotional Gift

Memoir of a Highly Sensitive Person Who Overcame Depression

Yong Kang Chan
www.nerdycreator.com

The Emotional Gift: Memoir of a Highly Sensitive Person Who Overcame Depression
Copyright © 2016 by Yong Kang Chan.

Disclaimer:
The conversations in the book all come from the author's recollections, though they are not written to represent word-for-word transcripts. Rather, the author has retold them in a way that evokes the feeling and meaning what was said and in all instances, the essence of the dialogue is accurate. Some names and identifying details have been changed to protect the privacy of individuals.

This book is not intended as a substitute for the medical advice of physicians. The author of this material makes no medical claims for its use. The material is not intended to treat, diagnose, advise about, or cure any illness. If you need medical attention, please consult with your medical practitioner.

Printed in the United States of America

First Edition, 2016

ISBN 978-981-09-8940-8

Cover illustrated by Rusty Doodle
Author photo by Benson Ang
Book edited by Jessica Bryan

Your Free Gifts

To thank you for purchasing my book, I've put together two free gifts for you.

Free Gift #1: Self-Love Quiz

Low self-esteem can lead to mental health such as depression or anxiety. After my recent episode of depression, I realize the importance of loving myself. So I created this free quiz on self-love to help others.

Do you love yourself unconditionally? Or are you too hard on yourself?

To find out more, please go to:

http://www.nerdycreator.com/self-love-quiz/

Free Gift #2: The Round Moon

The Round Moon is a short story (parable) about being different. Being an introvert and a highly sensitive person (HSP), I found it challenging to fit in sometimes.

This story was written to encourage us to embrace our differences and let our true beauty shine.

To download this FREE short story now, please go to:

http://www.nerdycreator.com/round-moon/

CONTENTS

Preface

If I had known depression would teach me something valuable about my life, I wouldn't have resisted it.

In fact, I would have welcomed it with open arms — or would I?

The two months I experienced depression were the darkest days of my life. I had no control over my tears. I couldn't sleep. I didn't have enough energy to accomplish anything. Sometimes, I couldn't even breathe properly because of panic attacks. It was as though someone or something had taken over my life and stolen my hope. Everything seemed pointless, colorless. I worried about the future much of the time and couldn't seem to do anything right. Suicidal thoughts were the worst. I wanted to get help but was afraid to let other people know. It was a scary and lonely experience.

But without depression, I would still be chasing a career that wasn't meant for me, and there wouldn't be this book or any future books written by me. The biggest challenge after writing a first book is writing a second one. After I published *Fearless Passion*, on September 2014, I toyed with the idea of writing another book. Maybe it would be a book to help creative people with their finances, or a guide for animators, or perhaps a book on self-publishing.

I had no lack of ideas, but I lacked courage. Ironic, isn't it? Especially when my first book is about finding the courage to do what we love. I had a lot of time to write my first book because I was unemployed. In contemplating a second book, I wasn't sure I could do it again; plus, there was the tedious process of publishing and marketing. Dreaming about writing was fun, but taking action? Perhaps another day. None of my ideas inspired me to write a second book—not until I became jobless and depressed again.

I felt compelled to write *The Emotional Gift*, not only because I survived depression but because it gave me the courage to write again. Depression made me realize *I am a writer,* and I need to own this identity. I had been dabbling at a few jobs, such as accounting and doing animation, but nothing was as satisfying as writing. I used to think I could be an entrepreneur who writes books occasionally to build my authority. Now, I know I am a writer who writes daily and happens to run a book business on the side. Writing always comes first. I had to experience depression in order to focus my priorities, and I'm grateful for the insight.

At first glance, *The Emotional Gift* seems like an evil sibling to *Fearless Passion*. The former is about depression, while the latter is about passion. The two books seem to represent good versus evil. Positive versus negative. Everyone wants to be happy. No one wants to feel depressed, or even talk about it. I thought so, too.

Depression helped me realize that life isn't all about being happy. *We can't have sunshine and no rain.* If passion is sunshine, then depression must be the rain. Rain isn't bad. It depends on the context. Sleeping at home when it's raining can be enjoyable, but camping outdoors when it's raining? Probably not. Depression isn't the adversary; similar to rain, it's just part of the journey.

Pretending to be passionate when we are truly depressed doesn't help. Numbing our feelings only makes things worse. Depression taught me to experience all of my feelings and not push them aside.

As a highly sensitive person, my biggest issue is anger. I have always believed it isn't nice to be angry with others. So I tend to ignore my anger whenever it arises, although this causes problems in the long run. I also tend to be self-sacrificing. Sometimes, I care more about what other people are feeling than what I feel myself. Depression reminded me that I need to check in with my own feelings more often.

My brother wasn't certain I should write this book. He thought it would be difficult to market, and that everyone would find out I'd been depressed. I also used to think I needed to protect myself and not show my vulnerability in front of others. But the truth is the more I hide my feelings, the more I allow feelings like shame to eat me up inside.

All of our experiences help us grow, whether they are positive or negative. *I believe I experienced depression so I could write about it and share the lessons I learned.*

My experience of depression was *emotional*, but it was also a *gift*. The best way to receive a gift is to accept it and be thankful, and I'm grateful for what depression has taught me.

Yong Kang Chan
Singapore
2016

Chapter 1

The Blindside

The moment I returned to Singapore and was welcomed by the haze, I knew something bad was going to happen.

I had been away from home for a month, living in Bali and attending *iLab,* a program for entrepreneurs. Bali felt different from Singapore. When I first arrived, I was uneasy, but in a good way. Never in my life had I felt so grounded and calm. It took a week to get used to it, but it was refreshing. In Bali, there were no worries about what to do next. I just followed the flow. Most nights, I would go to sleep at 10:00 p.m. when I was tired. Bali is a slow-paced, relaxing island with friendly people.

Singapore, on the other hand, makes you rush even when there is no need to rush. Living in Singapore for 31 years had made me immune to relaxation and peace. I didn't know how to take care of my body and check in with my feelings. Being busy is the norm in Singapore, so once I landed, I naturally got down to work.

On my way home from the airport in my dad's car, the first thing I did was send Jason a message. Jason is the founder of an animation studio in Singapore. We connected through LinkedIn. He wanted to meet me after reading my blog posts on animation because he found them interesting. Even though I had decided not to do animation anymore, Jason loved my intention of helping the animation industry grow. He is a veteran in the industry, and he wanted to help me get started. After our first long chat, I was surprised when he asked me to help out in his animation studio.

I was even more surprised when, after our second long chat, I agreed. I must have been starving myself of passion for the previous six months, because any "drop of water" that resembled passion looked like gold to me. I was so eager to help him that I promised to start work on October 5, 2015, the first workday after my return from Bali.

Just before I left for Bali, Jason was looking for a new place for his office. He needed to move because the government wanted to reclaim the building. I didn't want to turn up for work at an empty building, so I sent him a message to confirm the reporting time and venue:

Me: Hi Jason, I'm back in Singapore. Where should

I report for work on Monday? At 9:00 a.m.?

Jason: Not so soon. Thought we'd decide after we move to new office. I am flying to Indonesia next week, and I'm busy moving the office.

Not so soon? My heart froze when I saw his message. I thought we had agreed on a date. Why did he say it was not decided? Hadn't I written him a long email stating my decision to help him, what I could do, and how committed I was to work with him? I had even said explicitly that I would start on **October 5, 2015.** In bold! It wasn't that he hadn't read my email, because he replied saying how honored and excited he was to have me on board. He even wanted to meet me again to discuss his business model. So what happened?

My temperature rose and my blood began to boil. I hate it when my plans get screwed up. Plus, I'd left my contract job with HBO Asia so I could help Jason. I knew I couldn't control external factors and the actions of others, but still it was frustrating.

Instead of expressing my anger, I took
a deep breath and put aside my anger.
I simply suppressed it and told myself
all I needed was a solution to my
employment difficulties. Then,
everything would be fine.

From the various career and business books I have read, I've learned that instead of asking for a job or a favor, a person must first find a way to make a contribution. Even though I couldn't work with Jason full-time right now, I could definitely help ease his workload. He was always swamped with work. I could work part-time for him until he moved his office and settled down. I was even willing to help him for free during this period of transition. There must be something I could do for him.

Me: When will you be moving? I can help out if you want.

Jason: End November.

As much as I wanted to help him, I found it difficult to breathe when I saw those two words, "End November," because it meant no income for another two months. I hadn't earned a salary while I was in Bali, so now I would have no income for a total of three months! What was I going to do?

Usually, I wasn't that reckless. Previously, when I left my accounting job to finish studying animation, I had at least six months of income saved as a buffer. In fact, I had more than a year. But this time around, there was no buffer. I was so confident (or should I say blinded by my own optimism) that I had not planned for failure. If I had known there was a chance he would not hire me in October, I would have stayed with HBO Asia. I couldn't wait until the end November. I needed a part-time job soon.

Me: Hmm…do you need help on cash flow or other things first? If not, I'm going to find a two-month, part-time job.

Jason: Not for now, because I'm busy running around. Sorry for the misunderstanding. Are you completely done with HBO?

Me: Yeah, I left them in August.

Jason: Okay, *maybe* December. We will *try* to meet you after October 11th, when I get back. Let me talk to my wife, who is handling the accounts, to see if I can start you early if you cannot find a temp job. Sorry. Been overwhelmed with work, moving office, and coming events.

Me: Okay, sure. I can do more than just the accounts. If you are overwhelmed, perhaps I can help you research some possible sites, so when you come back you will have choices.

Jason: It's okay. I will lock down with the landlord on Monday.

I felt like my life was ruined. Jason had caught me by surprise, and I was unprepared. It was as though someone had hit me with a stick at the back of my head and I was left unconscious. Even though I had experience in finding new jobs, I knew how difficult it was being jobless—rather like trying to stay afloat in the water when you're sinking. The panic attacks and the anxiety. The difficulties in breathing. The struggles. It felt no different than drowning.

I had promised myself I would never experience this kind of situation again, but here I was, back in a familiar and insecure place.

Chapter 2

Not a Good Time to Make New Friends

The next day, when reality sank in, I decided to implement what I had learned from my entrepreneur program. To be positive and energized, I needed to connect with people who were already "in the flow" and making money. Working with entrepreneurs who had established ideas seemed like a good place to start.

However, I must have misinterpreted what was taught, because instead of connecting with people I already knew and had relationships with, I sought out strangers. The first week back, I contacted several random entrepreneurs from LinkedIn.

Something was really wrong with this idea!

First, why did I think LinkedIn was a good place to build relationships? I met Jason through LinkedIn and look what happened.

Second, I am an introvert. The extreme kind.

Networking has always been my weakness, the thing I hate to do the most. LinkedIn is a website based on the concept of networking and I was at my most vulnerable.

Third, people you meet online are unlikely to trust a stranger. They didn't know me or my abilities. As it turned out, I met Albert, who proved to be difficult.

To be fair, most of the people I met through LinkedIn were polite and kind, and it wasn't as if Albert was deliberately rude. It's just that he is an extreme extrovert, my total opposite. He doesn't filter what he says; I do. He's realistic; I'm an idealist. His main objective is to make money; my main objective is to inspire others. As a highly sensitive person, I just didn't like his attitude and the way he communicated.

***

When I first saw Albert's picture and read his profile description, I knew it was going to be a disaster. I try to avoid judging other people based on superficial first impressions, but something about Albert didn't feel right. He was hard to relate to. I was cringing inside, but I went ahead and initiated a meetup with him at his co-sharing workplace.

What was I thinking?

Oh how I wish I had listened to my intuition before engaging with Albert. Intuition has always been my greatest gift. It has provided me with many ideas for my creative work and saved me from a lot of trouble. It's just that when I feel stressed and desperate, I forget this gift.

Within less than a minute, I regretted starting a conversation with Albert. I love that everyone is different, but it drives me nuts when people are not open to any perspective other than their own.

The whole time I was with Albert, he did 95 percent of the talking. He spoke as though he was a teacher and I was a student who had made a mistake and needed to be scolded. Every time I tried to find common ground between us or share my point of view, he shot me down as though he was blowing a flying target out of the sky.

Albert has a background in human resources. When I told him about my job history as an accountant and animator, he immediately called me a "generalist" and a "scanner."

"Companies don't hire someone who is disloyal," he said. "You've been in and out of HBO Asia five times and keep changing your profession. Who wants an employee like that? Aren't you being vengeful for trying finding a part-time job now? Just because the animation studio founder didn't give you a job, you've decided to betray him. It seems very inconsiderate."

Albert seemed to think he was doing me a favor by giving me valuable human resource department advice, but all I could think was how judgmental he was. How dare he judge me when he didn't know me or the details of my employment history? A couple of times I went back to HBO Asia because they asked for help, and I couldn't just sit around and wait for Jason to hire me. What if he didn't? I still needed to feed myself and my family.

Why couldn't he see the situation from my perspective? Albert was definitely lacking in compassion for others.

I was pretty much done after that. I couldn't connect with him at all, and I didn't want to share any more of my personal details with him. I just wanted to get out of his office and end our conversation...immediately!

As I was trying to find a way to escape, Albert treated me to an apple from the pantry. A "poison" apple.

I knew he was a good negotiator and he was good at selling. I just didn't expect him to give me his standard sales pitch. His business linked part-time workers with employers, and he was in need of part-timers to supply his clients, so he tried to work his magic on me:

> **Albert:** The next time you meet up with someone, don't say you are trying to help them or that you can add value to their business, because it's not true. I've shared many tips about being an entrepreneur with you, but you have not shared anything with me.

> **Me** (feeling guilty): So what can I do for you?

> **Albert:** Well, you could start by introducing me to your bosses at HBO Asia.

No way was I going to recommend Albert to my managers at HBO Asia. He would most certainly ruin my relationships with them. I had gotten myself into this mess, and I wasn't going to pass it on to someone else!

> **Me** (in an attempt to reject him): They seldom hire part-timers. They prefer someone who can work full-time.

> **Albert** (knowing that it's not going to work): How

about this? You said you were willing to help me. I have a couple of clients in urgent need of customer service assistance. Why don't you help me with this? I don't hire people immediately. All of my staff have to work with my regular clients first. If you want to work for me, you will have to start out by taking a customer service job.

When did I say I wanted to work for him? I was only interested in meeting new people and exploring options, and I really didn't want to work for him. I had already told him I'm an extreme introvert. Customer service isn't something I enjoy, so why is he even asking? I was dying inside, but I continued trying to be as polite as possible.

Me (weak): I'm not good with customer service.

Albert (not backing down): The biggest resource you have right now is time. Since you are not working, this position would be a good source of income for you. If you want to be an entrepreneur, you need to try everything. I'm not asking you to be good with customer service. I'm asking you to go there and learn how to communicate with salespeople. You need to know how to communicate with your sales staff when you have a business.

It's undeniable that Albert is good at making deals. Every time I tried to run away, he blocked my path and backed me into a corner. He was smart, and he used the word "learn." He knew that learning is important to me and used it to convince me.

However, I don't like to make quick decisions. I need time alone to process information and the different options in any situation. I needed to sleep on his offer and consult my intuition. But, of course, Albert wasn't going to let me go until I agreed to work in customer service.

Me: I'll think about it.

Albert (threatens): If you want to be an entrepreneur, you must decide quickly. Send my staff a message right now and say you're interested in the job and that I recommended you.

I was weak and did what Albert ordered me to do.

Later, when his assistant didn't reply to my message, he even made me call the assistant. Afterwards, he told me I could leave. Manipulation might be a harsh word, but Albert did manipulate me into doing something I didn't want to do. He could tell I was accommodating and easy to bully, and he used it against me.

Albert enticed me to take a bite out of his poison apple — and I did.

***

The next day, I was disappointed with myself. Not only had I ignored my intuition and my feelings, I had continued the conversation because I am a pleaser. I didn't think it was nice to leave after a few minutes, especially when I was the one who had initiated the meetup.

I felt like a doormat. I hadn't stood up for myself when I should have. I didn't know when or how to say "no" to others, and I had allowed Albert to walk all over me like I was a child in primary or secondary school. I wasn't a kid or a teen anymore, so why didn't I stand up for myself and tell him firmly that I didn't want a customer service job?

I was supposed to start work that evening, but I

didn't want to go. However, I was afraid that if I didn't, he would say something nasty about me and make me feel even worse for breaking my promise. I knew that if I did what he wanted I wouldn't be true to myself and I would eventually quit.

I hate it when someone forces me to make a quick decision. It tells me they have no respect for me as a person. Being analytical and needing time alone to process information are part of my personality. If a person doesn't respect it, my answer should always be "No." It was obvious that I needed to learn how to reject others and stand up for myself.

So that morning, I stuck with my integrity and turned down his job offer. I felt a little relieved afterwards, but by that time I was already damaged.

Albert had opened up my deepest wound—the part of me that didn't feel worthy enough.

Chapter 3

I'm Not Worthy Enough

As I was on my way home from the airport, I told my family everything would be alright. After all, how hard could it be to find a new job? I had a degree in accounting and a diploma in animation. Yes, I hated to change my plans. But surely I could find something to feed myself. All I had to do was to find a part-time job for two months, and then join Jason's company in December. It didn't sound difficult.

At the time, I *really* thought I was fine. Until I discovered I was fine on the outside, but not on the inside.

Some days, I had panic attacks for no reason. I felt insecure and had trouble breathing. It was as though someone had put a gun to my head and I was going to die if I didn't get a job soon. Even though I tried to calm down with controlled, deep breathing, I couldn't help thinking about the terrible possibilities.

What if Jason didn't hire me in December? Re-

reading his messages definitely made me feel worse. He used noncommittal words such as "maybe" and "try."

"*Maybe* I will hire you in December," and "We will *try* to meet with you October 11th."

How could I be certain that when December came, he would actually hire me? I started thinking perhaps I should get a full-time job, instead.

But what if—like Albert said—no one would hire me? Would they think I'm fickle or weak-willed because I kept changing my profession?

What if I had no other choice but to go back to HBO Asia? What would my bosses, colleagues, family, and friends think of me?

"I told you so. The opportunity is not as good as it sounds."

"You're back again. Why don't you just stay here for good?"

"Don't you feel ashamed going back to HBO Asia so many times?"

What if I was forced to do accounts again? Every time I opened the online job search portal, I felt my nerves trembling. Sometimes I felt so desperate, I looked for jobs that were completely unsuitable. Other times, I read the job descriptions and told myself I wasn't good enough to be hired. After a while, I just stopped looking for a job because the search made me feel even more unworthy.

***

October 11th came, and there was no news from Jason. I could have contacted him instead, but my ego wouldn't let me. I didn't want to beg for a job. If he really needed me in his company, he would have already hired me. The fact that he hadn't hired me and even rejected my offer of free short-term help meant *I wasn't needed.*

Jason wasn't a bad person. He tried his best to help me get back into the animation industry by offering me a position in his company. We spent hours brainstorming the various positions that I was qualified for, and I did appreciate his positive intentions.

However, the more he tried to help me the less worthy I felt. I didn't want him to give me a job to the detriment of his company. If he decided to hire me, he should do it because he believed I would add value to his business. He shouldn't create a position just for me. Initially, he wanted me to be his accountant, but his wife was already doing the accounts. He justified this idea by saying it would allow her to take care of their child full-time. Sounds fair enough. But now that I think of it, his company wasn't doing that well, so wouldn't hiring me add stress to his financials? Plus, he had already told me there wasn't much accounting to be done because the company was small.

So why hire me?

In the past, I had earned the highest salary doing accounts, and he wanted me to have a good monthly income working for him. We spent many hours discussing what I could do, but nothing seemed to fit. Our discussions only made me feel worthless, as though I had nothing useful to contribute.

My self-worth was associated with what I could contribute. So was Jason's, and he couldn't stop helping me even though he knew it wasn't possible.

***

A person's self-worth doesn't get destroyed overnight by a couple of unexpected events. My sense of unworthiness started way back when I was a kid. I grew up in a typical Asian family in which praise and encouragement was scarce. When I achieved high scores on examinations, there was never any praise or reward from my parents. My dad, especially, was adamant not to give out acknowledgment for a job well done. It was as though scoring high marks was expected. So my mission as a kid was to achieve a perfect score and get the praise I deserved.

One day, I scored 100 marks on a mathematics test, and I couldn't wait to tell my dad. My expectations were high: *My dad will be so proud of me. He will think I'm smart and hardworking. He may even buy me something as a reward. Most importantly, he will finally praise me.*

I had a grin on my face as I imagined all the nice things that might happen.

I couldn't wait to hear what he was going to say. When I reached home and told my dad about my perfect score, I sat there waiting like a hungry puppy craving some delicious food.

But the first thing he said was, "The test must have been very easy."

The second thing he said was, "Many of the other students probably scored 100 marks, too, because it was so easy."

So instead of being praised, I was discredited. All my efforts to please him and make him proud were wasted. I was angry and disappointed, and deep down inside I felt unworthy. *It was as though no matter what I did, I would never be good enough.*

Chapter 4

Empathy Didn't Allow Me to Be Angry

Life has given me two wonderful gifts: intuition and empathy. Empathy is my good friend. She helps me connect with others by understanding what they are feeling. She has taught me how to love and be compassionate. I always enjoy watching a touching movie or singing an emotional song with her.

But sometimes, she makes me too soft. I can't watch violent or horror movies with her, because she makes me feel the pain the characters are experiencing. She tells me to think in terms of other people's perspectives, even when they treat me badly. Every time I am angry with someone and explode in front of them, she makes me repent and even cry.

Empathy is my good friend, but she doesn't allow me to be angry.

I didn't know what was wrong with me. Not only did I feel anxious during the day, I started waking up in the middle of the night and crying uncontrollably. So many emotions were emerging, and I didn't know what to do with them:

I felt unneeded. I always felt needed at HBO Asia. There was always a way to make a contribution. But even so, the last time I went back I didn't feel welcome anymore—and now, Jason didn't need me, either.

I felt betrayed. I signed up for one of Jason's courses because he said it would help me understand the animation industry and his company better. I wasn't interested at first, but I was really looking forward to joining his company, so I signed up. I couldn't help but feel resentful at the way things turned out.

I felt hopeless. Would I be able to survive without HBO Asia? If no other company would hire me, there was no other choice but to go back to them.

I felt shame. I had already worked at HBO Asia five times. I didn't want to go there again, especially when I had left the company for something "better." If I returned again, I would probably die of shame.

I felt insecure. I had less and less money as the days passed. What if I had to sell my stocks at a loss? What if Jason never hired me? What if I couldn't get another job, and soon?

I felt lost. Should I be an animator or accountant again? I had already decided I didn't want to do animation or accounting anymore. Should I work at something I don't like just to feed myself?

I felt afraid. Why was I crying uncontrollably all the time? Why was I experiencing so many emotions? What was happening to me?

Unlike how nicely these emotions are presented here, my emotions were out-of-control. There were so many different voices in my head talking at the same time. Was I going crazy? It was like playing the arcade game *Whac-A-Mole*. When I hit and pressed an emotion down with the mallet, another one popped up from a separate hole. The more I *resisted* my feelings, the more they emerged to the surface and lingered. I totally sucked at this "game." But it was not a game at all; it was a very serious situation.

As the nights went by, I started feeling more and more frustrated. Why wouldn't the emotions simply go away? I just wanted to sleep in peace. Then, as though things couldn't get any worse, a new and destructive set of emotions began to challenge me: revenge, hatred, jealousy, and rage, or, in short, anger.

Anger wasn't like the other emotions I had experienced. "He" wasn't soft. He had arrived with a vengeance, and he was ready to make a statement. The first thing he did was make sure I understood that this whole mess wasn't my fault; it was Jason's fault. Jason was the cause of the disruption in my life and the resulting misery.

If Jason hadn't asked me to work for him, I would still be working at HBO Asia. If Jason hadn't told me how much I could contribute to the animation industry, I wouldn't have been so optimistic about helping him. If Jason had told me sooner that he wasn't going to hire me on October 5, 2015, I would have found another job in Bali.

Anger tried to help me feel better about myself by pushing the blame onto someone else, but there were issues. When Anger took over, sometimes I blew up. Even though it's rare, when it happens it can be destructive and result in many casualties.

My good friend Empathy never liked Anger.

After each explosion, she would say something like, *See what Anger has done to the people around you. Do they deserve to be the objects of your frustration? If you were on the receiving end, how would you feel?*

When Empathy helped me understand the pain my anger caused others, I cried. She was right. They didn't deserve to be hurt like that. No one deserves abuse. It was my fault. I should have controlled my anger better and communicated my boundaries more clearly.

When Anger came back this time around, Empathy was at the door ready to stop him from creating any harm. She asked me to look at the situation from Jason's perspective and understand what he was going through:

Jason was just trying to help you get back into animation. He saw your passion to help the industry and wanted to give you an opportunity. He didn't want things to end up like this. He was given a short notice by the government to move. It was stressful for him, too. He needed to spend money to renovate the new place and make time to communicate with the contractors. He might have forgotten to contact you because he was busy moving his office. Try to empathize with him and see the situation in terms of his perspective.

Yes, I would definitely try.

I tried to convince myself it wasn't *right* to be angry with Jason. He was doing the best he could. If I were in his position, I would be stressed, too. I should give him some time to settle his problems.

Empathy didn't want me to be angry. So I wasn't. Every time Anger came back, I just pushed it aside and pretended it didn't exist.

But what about the other emotions: feeling unneeded, betrayed, hopeless, full of shame, insecure, lost, and afraid? Should I numb them, too? Was it even possible?

Chapter 5

The Untold Story of *Fearless Passion*

Crying at night was really getting to me. I couldn't focus during the day. Empathy was very good at stopping Anger, but not good with other emotions. I felt drained from having so many intense feelings and just wanted to lie on my bed and do nothing.

However, my emotions weren't going to let me escape that easily. Once Empathy had stopped me from feeling angry towards Jason, I had no one else to blame *but myself*. So my emotions began to attack me, instead. They said hurtful, nasty things in my head:

You can't blame Jason for betraying you, if you are naive enough to believe what he says.

Do you think HBO Asia still wants you back? You aren't welcome there.

Don't even try to find a new job. No one is going to hire you.

You're a loser. You can't even deal with your own feelings.

Give up your dreams. Whatever you strive for is not going to work.

You are worthless.

I couldn't stand what the voices were saying, but I couldn't do anything about it. I tried numbing them out — it didn't work. I tried distracting myself with TV shows — it didn't last. I tried ignoring them — they kept coming back. I felt powerless, trapped, and exhausted. I didn't have the energy to fight and resist my emotions anymore, so I just laid in my bed and let them belittle me. Slowly, I started believing what they said. Maybe I wasn't going to find a job I could love. Maybe it was time to give up my dreams and accept reality. Maybe I should just go back to being an accountant.

I was *hopeless*.

I was in *pain*.

I had no *choice*.

Suddenly, a scary yet familiar thought flashed in my mind — *Kill yourself. The only way to stop the pain is to kill yourself. It will set you free.*

This wasn't the first time I'd had suicidal thoughts. The last time was seven years before, when I was an auditor. It was long before I wrote my first book *Fearless Passion* and became committed to pursuing my passion. Many people had observed my career change from accounting to animation and thought it was courageous, but most of them didn't know what was behind my decision.

***

Auditing was my first job out of university and I hated that job, although I didn't know why. Most of the auditors I knew also hated their jobs, so I thought it was normal. But now, in hindsight, I realize that being an auditor didn't fit my personality at all.

Every morning, when I walked through the subway to my office, I became lost in the black and white. My office was located in the financial district of Singapore, and it was crowded in every direction. Everyone was busy and rushing around. Every day, I saw white-collar workers smoking their life away outside the tall buildings. It was all about stress, frustration, and unhappiness. There was no color, no joy, no love. If I hadn't been so sensitive to the environment, I would probably still be there. But I was sensitive, and seeing zombie-like people each day brought up too much sadness. I just wasn't suited to work in a corporate environment.

There was no meaning in my job.
Helping others is meaningful. Sharing
insights is meaningful. Seeing people
grow is meaningful. Checking for
compliance as an auditor? Boring.
Even though I obeyed the rules, that
doesn't mean I had to love enforcing
them.

When I was in primary two, my form teacher asked me to keep the class quiet between lessons. Big mistake! I might have been a quiet student, but I didn't know how to keep the class quiet. I just stood still in front of the class trying to focus on who was making noise. Later, when the next teacher came, she told everyone to not make noise, otherwise they would be punished and made to stand in front of the class like me. I was shocked and embarrassed. I'd been appointed to keep the class quiet, but she assumed I was a troublemaker and shamed me for it.

Most people didn't know I cared little about compliance. Sure, I followed the rules, but I was always on the lookout for ways to change the rules and make life easier and more fun. I didn't enjoy copying what was done previously by our audit seniors. My real love was being creative and coming up with my own insights. Checking the clients for compliance didn't feel right. I was more interested in talking with them and understanding the hardships they faced as accountants.

Basically, I was a bad auditor.

The senior bosses thought I wasn't aggressive enough with the clients. They wanted me to ask more questions. On the other hand, I felt the clients didn't want to be bothered, because they had their own work to do. So most of the time, I would read up and find the answers on my own first, consolidate my questions, and then schedule time with my clients. Because of this, I was deemed passive at work.

All I wanted to do was help, not regulate. I didn't like working in an environment that was filled with animosity. The clients had their defenses up, and they weren't willing to share information with us. They were afraid we would find their mistakes. The seniors were fighting over manpower so they could have smooth-sailing engagements. Everyone was looking out for themselves.

I needed harmony.

After a year, I'd had enough. The long working hours, the stressful deadlines, and the uncooperative work environment were taking a toll. Long hours of doing something I hated was affecting my physical and mental health. I was exhausted from work and not getting enough sleep at night. There was no peace because I kept thinking about the nightmares I would have to face the next day. There was no motivation to go to work in the morning because I didn't know what I was working *for*.

I started sinking into fear and negativity.

One day, while at a client's office, I nearly had a breakdown. I couldn't bring myself to switch on my laptop. I stared at the blank screen for a few minutes. The thought of switching on the laptop made me want to cry. I was paralyzed because I hated my job but was afraid to leave. I was afraid I wouldn't be able to find another job and I would have no income. I didn't want to disappoint my parents and colleagues. My parents would worry if I left my current job without a replacement and my colleagues would have to do my crap if I quit.

It was like being confined in a small box with no way out. I didn't want to stay in my existing job, but I couldn't leave, either. I didn't know what was happening to me, and I was overwhelmed with emotions. I felt I had no choice and control over my life. I started becoming *hopeless*, and it was so bad I wanted to end my life.

***

Dreaming about the future and being creative; creating a vision and exploring ideas; this is what I valued and loved. To others, it might seem overly idealistic, but this was my identity, who I am. Dreaming gave me hope. Without dreams, I felt hopeless and lacking a strong sense of self-identity. People had no idea how important my vision was to me. To be hopeless and be told to give up my dreams is the same as telling me to give up my *self* and not be me. It's like telling me to go away and die.

I had lost my ability to see hope, and that's why I

had suicidal thoughts.

Chapter 6

Is This Depression?

I wasn't sure I was having a depression. My emotions were beating me inside out and upside down. I was crying a lot for no reason, and I didn't have the energy to do anything. Sometimes, I wanted to end my life. Were these symptoms of depression? What is depression?

As an empathetic person, it was easy for me to feel what other people were feeling. But when it came to my own feelings, I had no idea what they were and how to deal with them. There were times when I wasn't even sure they were my own feelings. Sometimes, it seemed I unintentionally picked up the emotions of strangers on the road, which is one of the biggest drawbacks about being a highly sensitive person.

Having had a similar experience seven years previously helped me understand what was going on. I felt the same hopelessness and powerlessness, except this time with more intensity.

When I was an auditor, I didn't know depression was slowly creeping up on me. All I knew was I didn't want to get up in the morning, I was holding back my tears and felt like dying. Even though I had suicidal thoughts, I didn't think it was anything serious because I didn't believe I would actually kill myself.

Now, reflecting back on the situation, I feel really lucky. I didn't make any effort to heal myself, but something at work saved me. When I was returning from lunch one day, I saw one of my female colleagues rushing out of the client's office and into the women's restroom with tears in her eyes. I didn't know why she was crying, but seeing someone else who going through a similar experience was powerful. It shifted my perspectives and I started asking questions:

- Why do we force ourselves to do something we hate?
- Why do we exchange our happiness for money?
- Why do we allow ourselves to be so miserable?
- Why is there so much crying at work?
- Why is everyone so stressed out?

I couldn't understand my own feelings, but when I saw my colleague cry I could relate to her's. This gave me the energy to take action on my own problems. I started reading books and finding career information online. I wanted to know what jobs suited my personality. What am I passionate about? How can I work at something I love? I renewed my goals and vision about the future. Most importantly, I realized there is hope, and this saved me from sinking further into the darkness.

But was I depressed? It wasn't serious enough that I needed to see a doctor or take medicine. Was I exaggerating my emotions? However, if I hadn't seen my colleague cry would I have become hopeless to the point of no return? Would I have killed myself?

Am I having a depression now?

Both times I believed I was depressed. The first time, it was mild, and it was resolved before I could even react to it. This time, my feelings were more intense because I wasn't working, and I was home all day trying to deal with my emotions.

I also read articles and watched videos to confirm I was having depression. Here is a list of the symptoms I discovered:

- No energy and interest in doing things
- Feeling hopeless and helpless
- Recurring thoughts of death and suicide
- Difficulty concentrating and making decisions
- Insomnia
- A sense of restlessness and tiredness
- Feeling worthless and bad about yourself
- Desire to be alone and not interact with others
- Significant weight loss or weight gain
- Aches and pains

Other than the last two points listed above, I had all of the symptoms of depression. I am not a doctor, but my research and intuition showed me that I was depressed.

Depression is not the same as sadness. Most people think they are the same, but they aren't. We can feel sad when we end a relationship, lose a job, or have a critical illness, but that doesn't necessarily mean we are depressed.

When we are depressed, we believe there's no hope. No matter what we do, we believe nothing is going to change, nothing is going to work, and nothing we do matters. We don't just feel sad because a relationship has ended; we believe we will never find someone to love again. We don't just lose a job; we believe no one will ever hire us. We don't just have a critical illness; we believe there is no cure for our illness, so why bother living.

Depressed people have no hope. It's as though someone hit them on the back of the head with a stick and the muscle called "hope" snapped. They are not lacking hope in just one aspect of their life, but usually every aspect of life: career, finance, relationships, health, and creativity. They live with tremendous fear and insecurity about the future. They feel powerless and trapped in the moment, and they want to die because they want to end the pain.

Scientifically, depression is a brain disorder. Studies show that repetitive bouts of depression cause the hippocampus to shrink. The hippocampus is located in the temporal lobe of the brain, the area associated with memory recall and emotions. Damaging it can result in the loss of memory and difficulty in forming new memories.

However, reading scientific studies didn't help much. I was too depressed to decipher what the scientific terms meant, and the more I read them the more afraid I became. How could I afford to see a doctor and get treated when I was jobless? So I stopped reading the scientific studies altogether.

Now that I knew I had depression and understood it more, what could I do about it?

Chapter 7

Wandering Is Healing

Some days, I hoped the nightmare wasn't real. I wanted to be back in Bali, learning about entrepreneurship and enjoying the sunlight. I didn't want to be in foggy, rainy Singapore.

The good thing about having been through depression once is that I was more aware of my situation this time. I knew I needed to find a way to feel better, but I just didn't know how. I knew I couldn't keep forcing myself to look for a new job because it had already proven to cause more misery. Plus, I wasn't in a good enough emotional state to make the effort. My well-being was more important than finding a new job or feeling financially secure. So I stopped focusing on what I *had* to do, and listened to what my soul *needed,* instead.

One morning, I woke up feeling exhausted, both physically and mentally. My emotions had been tormenting me the whole night and I couldn't sleep. I was sick of being in the same place. It was like being sentenced to jail for not knowing how to deal with depression. I needed a new environment. I needed to get away from the people I knew. I needed to move, escape, and hide from my present reality.

All I needed was to get out of my house and go somewhere. Anywhere!

Right after breakfast, I packed my bag, let my elder brother know I was having a bad day, and left the house. This day was only going to be about me, no one else. There would be no worrying about what the future held. There would be no worrying about my responsibility towards my parents. There would be no worrying about my depression getting better or worse. I just wanted a quiet space and time for myself.

But I didn't know where to go, so I just let my foot lead the way.

I told my foot, *Go wherever you want to go. You are free now. Roam.* When I reached a bus stop and a bus arrived, I simply boarded the bus. I didn't care where it was going, as long as it took me far away from home.

There is something carefree about wandering. Having no direction can be the best direction. It reminded me *I had choices in life.* I could choose which bus to take and also where to get off. It was all up to me. We are always so busy worrying about our troubles that we let them consume us. If we just take some time off to relax and be in the moment, we can be as carefree as we want to be. All our worries and anxieties about the future are really "much ado about nothing."

I chose to stay on the bus until it reached the end of the line—all the way to the Tampines Bus Interchange. I hadn't taken the time to touch base with my emotions because I was busy fighting reality and building a career. The long bus ride allowed me to journal about my situation. Those blank pieces of paper gave me space to process and express my feelings without being judged, and seeing new scenery out of the window offered new perspectives.

But expressing my feelings on paper wasn't easy. My emotions were more intense than what I could describe in words. Feelings are incoherent, by their very nature, and they are difficult to describe. Acknowledging my emotions was also difficult. I didn't want to relive the pain I had experienced during the previous nights. It was unbearable. My thoughts were unforgiving when it came to criticizing my failures and mistakes.

However, I knew it was essential.

For the past seven years, I had invested

considerable time on personal growth. One technique I love is called the Sedona Method. Instead of expressing or repressing our feelings, the Sedona Method suggests we welcome our feelings and then let them go. Letting go of emotions isn't difficult if we understand we can be detached from our emotions. It's like dropping a pen we hold in our hand. Anyone can do it.

Pixar's 2015 animated feature *Inside Out* also helped me understand the importance of not denying my feelings. The movie is about a happy, eleven-year-old girl named Riley, who moves from Minnesota to San Francisco with her parents. Instead of telling the story from Riley's perspective, the story is told from the perspective of Riley's dominant emotion, Joy. Together with Joy, Riley's other emotions—Sadness, Anger, Disgust, and Fear—influence how she acts and help her cope with her new environment. The problem arises when Joy tries to prevent Sadness from causing Riley to feel sad. Even though the movie never once mentions the word "depression," it taught me that suppressing emotions is unhealthy. All emotions are important and useful. Numbing any of them can eventually lead to depression.

I couldn't believe I had forgotten what I had already learned. All this time, I had been numbing my emotions instead of *letting them be*. I had forgotten that the more I prevent myself from feeling pain, the more I am doomed to struggle with it. The more I ran away and ignored my emotions, the more they stuck with me. This reminds me of when I was in Bali. Some friends were teaching me how to swim, and whenever I panicked and struggled in the water, I sank. However, when I relaxed and felt the currents in the water, I floated. Held in the grip of suffering, I couldn't separate myself from my emotions.

I mistakenly believed that I was my emotions.

Instead of making judgmental statements about myself and my feelings, I started talking to myself with empathy, as though I was talking to a friend: *I'm sorry I denied your emotions and made them seem unimportant. When you are willing to share, I'll be here to listen.*

I asked myself questions such as:

- How are you doing?

- What's wrong?
- What happened?
- Why do you feel this way?

Listening without judgment, I allowed myself to be as honest as possible with my feelings and wrote down whatever came to my mind—all the betrayal, anger, and unworthiness. Having this outlet to express my emotions and pour my heart out helped me feel a lot calmer.

But, unfortunately, it didn't last.

At the end of my day of wandering, my foot brought me to Changi Airport, which is a nice place to be if you are going for a holiday. As I looked at all the happy travellers with envy, I thought, *How nice it would be to leave Singapore right now and be away from the nightmare of my life*, even though I knew in my heart that leaving town would not solve my inner difficulties with depression.

Chapter 8

The Problem with Asking for Help

After writing down my feelings, I still felt rather unsettled. Perhaps it was because I was outside. Even though I felt like crying, I held back my tears. Crying in public or in front of others was the *last thing* I wanted to do. Just recently, in Bali, I had a breakdown in front of everyone while talking about having low self-esteem as a kid. I would not allow myself to be embarrassed like that again.

But this wasn't a time for denial. I needed help desperately. I needed to get back to a balanced and positive state of mind. There were many things I had planned to do after I came back from Bali.

I read that one of the best ways to stop feeling depressed is to share your feelings with someone who is supportive. However, the biggest obstacle I had was opening up. Showing the most vulnerable aspects of myself to others was nerve-racking and humiliating. It was easy to share my story when I had overcome an adversary, but to share my story when I was still trying to reach resolution? No way! No one wants others to see their open wounds.

Another big problem I had with asking for help is that not everyone understands depression. Most people who have not experienced it believe that as long as they think positively everything will be fine. Being positive is healthy, and there is a time for positive thinking, but for me this wasn't the time.

Telling a person who is depressed to have positive thoughts is the same as telling a sick person not to be sick. It doesn't work.

No one can control or stop specific thoughts from entering his or her mind. We can rephrase our thoughts to be more positive, but we can't stop them from being negative, and even if depressed people do have positive thoughts, they don't always believe they are true.

Depressed people have no hope. They only see the negative and are unable to recognize the positive. They don't believe something positive can actually happen to them.

It's not as though depressed people don't want to be helped. We need help. We are just so *hopeless* sometimes that we don't believe seeking support will change anything. Plus, it's important to get help from the right person. Otherwise, our difficulties can get worse.

I didn't know how to seek help, or from whom. I didn't want to see a doctor. First, it was costly. Second, I didn't want my family to know about my depression. Previously, when I told my parents being an auditor made me want to die, they didn't offer any love or support. Instead, they reprimanded me for being foolish and not recognizing the effort and time they had put in to raise me and the pain they would feel if I died. Basically, they thought only of themselves.

Furthermore, I was too ashamed to ask for help, so I decided to try and heal myself. I would not ask for help, but would seek help online instead:

1. Watching documentary shows about depression and reading other people's stories in forums was helpful. It was great to know others were going through the same experience, but it made me more

depressed because it seemed they all felt trapped, helpless, and wanted to end their lives, too.

2. I watched videos on yoga. I had practiced yoga three times a week in Bali, and it helped me feel more centered, so I thought it might help with depression. But it didn't. I stopped doing it after a while because I woke up feeling drained every day. I didn't have the energy and focus to practice yoga regularly.

3. I listened to music, watched TV shows, and played mindless games online. These activities distracted me for a while. But after some time, I would get depressed again for no apparent reason.

4. I listened to some self-help audio I had purchased previously, but it wasn't as effective as before. My emotions were so intense that I couldn't concentrate on them. It was as though some part of me was rejecting anything that might be helpful.

All the information I gathered would have been useful *if* I was already on the way to recovery, but not now, when I was still so deeply depressed. However, one piece of information did manage to sneak past my emotional upheaval and go straight into my consciousness and heart.

Chapter 9

I Had Failed Miserably

Nothing seemed to work. I decided to give up healing and focus on finding a job. If I could find a job and get paid, maybe my problem with depression would disappear and I would feel better. But rather than staying at home to do the job search, this time I went to a co-working space near my home to write my resume. Perhaps a change of environment would be good.

After applying for several jobs in the morning, I was getting bored and impatient. To distract myself from feeling emotionally unstable again, I began to watch some random videos on YouTube. When I reached Dr. Brené Brown's Ted Talk entitled "Listening to Shame," I fell apart.

Yes, it was a public breakdown—*the last thing* I wanted to do.

As I watched the video, I couldn't stop sobbing. I was a mess. I was running out of tissue paper. It was so bad I had to pause the video to breathe. I was definitely embarrassed! A 31-year-old guy crying for no apparent reason in public! Luckily, I had a tiny cubicle in the co-working space. I lowered my head and kept my crying volume down so other people wouldn't see my puffy eyes or hear me weeping. I didn't want anyone to think I was a nutcase or come up to me and ask, "How are you?" I would bury myself in shame if someone did that. How ironic was this, considering I had just watched a video that encourages people to pay attention to shame.

What was wrong with me? I had watched the video several times before. It's a great video and I love it, but I didn't recall it being a trigger for a breakdown. It was supposed to be a funny yet informative talk about shame. I guessed I never truly understood what Dr. Brené Brown meant until I watched it this time.

As I tried to calm down in my cubicle at the co-work space, I realized I had been living in shame for the past year. I was ashamed of myself because of my book, *Fearless Passion*. Most people probably believe that being an author is something to be proud of, but I wasn't proud.

In my book, I wrote about my journey from being an accountant to learning animation. But after three months of being an animator, I discovered making animation wasn't my passion. When my contract ended, I decided not to do it anymore. Since then, I had made no effort to market my book. It wasn't because I didn't have the time or the know-how. The truth was I felt embarrassed to promote the book. I felt like a fraud because I had failed to do what my book encouraged.

Who am I to talk about passion when I'm not even doing something I'm passionate about?

It wasn't easy to make the decision to quit being an animator. I had left my home and family in Singapore to pursue an animation career in Malaysia. I had also left a high-paying position for a job that barely covered the cost of food. I felt strongly about my career choice, even though my family didn't support it. I had given up everything to pursue my dream, but the dream turned out to be nothing like what I had envisioned.

Who am I?

What should I do for gainful employment?

Be an accountant again?

Find other jobs for which I was not qualified?

I was left with no identity.

What would other people think if I stopped being an animator? Would my friends and readers, who admired my courage, think I'm the type of person who gives up easily? Would they think I'm a failure? Would my dad say,

"I told you so?"

But if I continued doing animation, I wouldn't be practicing what my book preaches: *follow your passion, but don't follow your passion blindly.* My intuition told me animation wasn't the right field for me. If I continued doing it, wouldn't I be lying to myself? Could I ever be happy living a life of delusion and denial?

It took two weeks to make the decision. I didn't want to announce to the world that I was a failure, so I took the *middle ground approach.* I wrote a lengthy blog post to explain that giving up animation *was* being true to myself. I found excuses to justify why I wasn't contradicting my book. I even said I would eventually come back to the animation industry. Not once did I mention the word "failure" in my post. Basically, I wasn't committed to anything. I had put one foot in the animation industry and left one foot out, just in case. All I knew was I didn't want to be humiliated.

However, by not admitting my failure my shame grew even stronger. After my animation job, I returned to HBO Asia for the fifth time to help them with their accounting systems. During the six months back at HBO Asia, I almost wanted to dig a hole and put my head into it. Everyone thought I was pursuing my passion in animation.

Now, they knew that I had failed.

I cried so hard while I was in the co-working cubicle, because I realized I had made a huge mistake. I had wasted a year of my life living a lie. Shame had caused me to make the wrong decisions and led me in an unproductive direction:

- I thought I needed to start a business related to animation, but this decision restricted my growth.
- I studied coding, thinking I could build a platform for animators.
- I jumped at the opportunity to help Jason and the animation industry, even as my feelings were screaming that something was wrong.
- I wrote blog posts about animation resources, even though they weren't the type of posts I love writing.

For the past year, I had limited myself by thinking I needed to associate with the field of animation. There were signs everywhere telling me I was going down the wrong path, but I refused to acknowledge them. Subconsciously, I must have been thinking that if I went back to the animation industry sometime in the future, then I would be able to promote my book again and not be considered a failure. When Jason didn't hire me, my whole world came crashing down because I realized I wasn't going back to the animation industry. It wasn't just a job I was losing, I was being tagged a failure (by myself). I didn't want to admit I was wrong about my passion, but it was costly because I had to surrender my authentic self to shame. Shame — according to what Dr. Brené Brown said in the video — is highly correlated with depression and suicidal feelings.

"Vulnerability is not weakness. Vulnerability is pure courage. Life is about daring greatly." These words from Dr. Brené Brown offered such great encouragement. Even though I know it's impossible to succeed without failing, she taught me that *being successful without honoring failure is not a true representation of the journey*. She's right about it; there is no story to tell when everything is perfect. Most movies have characters who struggle and fail in one way or another. It's called being human.

Fearless Passion isn't all about passion. I had forgotten my book is about courage, too. I might not be doing something passionate right now, but I did have the courage to start over again. Even though I decided to turn away from a career in animation, I had other passions to pursue. It wasn't the end of the world.

Someone can take away my job, but they can only take away my courage if I let them.

I had the most liberating and rewarding cry ever in public. Failure and shame had held me back from moving forward, but Dr. Brené Brown's video had given me new hope.

Chapter 10

Being Vulnerable

When I was in Bali, one mentor gave each of us something to work on when the program was complete and we returned home. She was absolutely right about mine. The first thing I was instructed to work with was to accept the idea that *I'm worthy enough*. Not just being okay with myself, but really loving and being fully happy with who I am. The second thing was to *open up and share my vulnerabilities*. This wasn't about being extroverted; it was about love and connection.

In the past, I'd had a tendency to shut myself off from the world for protection. I didn't want others to know I was sensitive and that I didn't feel good about myself. I didn't think anyone would care about what I had to share. This was especially true when I was a teen in secondary school. I attended an all-boy school. The other kids were more active and outgoing, while I prefer to read and spend time alone.

I thought I had overcome my low self-esteem issues as an adult, but this depression episode proved I wasn't as free from it as I thought. There was still a part of me that was unloving towards myself, and it was capable of exploding into something quite detrimental.

I'm an introvert and good at keeping everything to myself. But this way of being has always prevented me from receiving the love and connection I crave. No one in my family ever talked about feelings. I don't know if this is an Asian cultural trait, or whether my family members simply preferred to keep their feelings to themselves. From a young age, I needed someone to share my feelings with comfortably, but there wasn't anyone I trusted. So I wrote my feelings down on paper, which helped a lot.

Writing helped me survive my darkest time in the past.

But this time, I was too deep in depression and couldn't focus on writing.

How else could I express my feelings?

***

The next day, after crying in the co-working space, my elder brother and I had lunch together in front of the

TV, as usual. He must have noticed that I haven't been myself lately, because he asked, "How are you doing?"

Even though I had been depressed for almost a month, I had managed to hide it from my family. I would do most of my crying at night, or shut my door and pretend I was working on a project when I needed to cry. Sometimes, I would just sleep on my bed and do nothing, or I would go out if I was feeling really awful. To have my elder brother notice something wasn't quite right was a surprise and it meant a lot.

So…I broke down…again.

I didn't want to express my vulnerability in front of my family. I didn't want them to know. First, I didn't think they would understand the experience of depression. My parents had brushed me off years ago when I told them I was depressed. I didn't want them to worry. Second, I felt rather ashamed of letting others know I had depression. I wanted to fix the problem on my own and continue as though nothing had happened, just like the last time.

However, it wasn't possible. My depression was getting too severe. I couldn't do it by myself—and the Universe didn't want me to do it by myself, either. She sent Dr. Brené Brown's video and my mentor to remind me that I needed to *open up and be vulnerable.* I was beginning to learn that I shouldn't let shame take control of my life and stop me from receiving the support I needed.

Tears rolled down my eyes, but I couldn't speak. I didn't know what to say. My elder brother was taken aback by the tears. Not knowing what else to do, he handed me a piece of tissue and waited patiently for me to stop crying.

Luckily, my parents were in the kitchen preparing to leave the house. With my back facing them, I simply ate my lunch and said goodbye when they left, pretending that everything was normal. Only my elder brother could see the tears in my eyes and the tissue in my hand.

After my parents left, I cried for a good two to three minutes, while my elder brother handed me tissues. When I started to calm down, I told him, "I don't know why I'm crying so much lately. Everything seems to be falling apart. I'm afraid of the future."

"What are you afraid of?" he said.

"I'm afraid that I won't have enough money. I didn't put any aside when I left HBO Asia to work in animation. I thought I would begin working with Jason when I came home from Bali."

"How many months of savings do you have left?" said my brother.

"Two to three more months before I will need to sell

my investments at a loss." I felt ashamed to admit that I hadn't saved much money before changing jobs.

"It's okay. You can always cut down your expenses or delay your allowance to our parents. Dad won't let you sell your investments at a loss, anyway, and in the meantime you can look for a job." My brother was trying to reassure me.

"But it's not just about the money. I feel lost and useless, and like I have no future. Doing accounting and animation feels like a death sentence. I cannot switch to another field, because then I'd need to further my studies, and further studying would mean I'd need more money. I have never regretted studying accounting and animation, but now I regret my career choices. I feel like I'm trapped in jail and can't break free."

I was thankful he cared enough to check in with me. My elder brother didn't quite understand depression, but he did try to help me see possibilities. He helped renew my hopes for the future by going through alternative career options with me. This gave me new ideas about how to follow my passion. He reminded me of all the great things I had done so far and encouraged me to move forward when I got stuck or overly analytical.

Most importantly, I felt more connected with him

after I shared my emotions.

I didn't have to hide anymore, at least not from him — or Jason.

Chapter 11

What Happened When Anger Fought Back

Crying wasn't enough to get rid of depression. I had cried for two days in public, but my depression still wasn't going away. Then I stumbled upon an article that said not to give someone who is crying a tissue because it will stop them from crying. Instead, allow the person to fully express his or her emotions. I had tissues with me every time I cried. Perhaps it was time to let myself go and try crying out all my tears.

Although crying was relatively easy, I had major problems with Anger. My friend Empathy had been pushing Anger to the side all the while, and, of course, Anger didn't like it. He needed some attention and expression, too. The more Empathy pushed him away, the stronger Anger became. He wasn't going to back down without a fight. Like the other emotions, he kept looping the same stories in my head like a broken record.

Story #1: *Maybe.* What did Jason mean when he used this word? Maybe he will hire you, or maybe he will *not* hire you? Don't take "maybe" for an answer. It's either "yes" or "no." Let Jason know you are done with him. Go get another job, instead. There are better jobs out there.

Story #2: *We will try to meet you.* This obviously means we will meet you *if* we have the time or *when* we feel like it. If Jason really wanted to meet you, he would have called already, or at least made an effort to schedule a time.

Story #3: If Jason really wanted to help you, he wouldn't have blindsided you. Why do you care so much about his feelings when he doesn't care about yours?

Even more "stories" were added to the "playlist" when I received more messages from Jason. On October 27, 2015, he contacted me about the change of dates for his course. He told me he would be heading to China on November 7th and would *try* to catch up with me before he left.

But Anger was still very sensitive regarding his use of the word "try."

> **Story #4:** *Try.* See what I told you? Do you seriously believe he will schedule a meeting with you? You are always scheduling meetings with him. When did he ever schedule a meeting with you?

Anger was right. Jason always talked about meeting, but he never once arranged a specific time. I always took the initiative to schedule our meetings. If he was serious about having me in his company, he would have made the effort. Why did I always have to be the one to do it? This time, I was adamant not to initiate the meetup.

On November 2nd, he messaged me again, and it wasn't to schedule a meetup. It was to change the dates for his course *again*. This time, Anger was really in an uproar.

> **Story #5:** Why is everyone expected to work around Jason's schedule? Why do you have to bow down to him and change your schedule to fit his? You're the one who paid for the course. How can

you work with someone who is so uncommitted?

Anger made a compelling case. Could I work with someone who was as unpredictable as Jason? His adaptive nature made me feel quite insecure. His strength was basically my weakness—I couldn't handle change and uncertainty very well. On paper, people with different personalities should complement each other and work well together, but it wasn't like that with Jason. His inability to make a commitment was intolerable.

Empathy had always been my strength. She had helped me with a lot of things, but not this time.

This time, Anger had won the war.

***

One day, as I wandered around the city, I listened to a self-help recording by Jack Canfield, the author of *Chicken Soup for the Soul*. In one of the tracks, he mentions the Emotional Scale. This "scale" shows what level of emotions applies to you. He said emotions are just energy. At the higher levels, they have more vibrational energy. So the higher the level you are, the greater the vibrational energy you will experience.

This makes sense. On the Emotional Scale, depression is at Level 1 and anger is at Level 2, which means anger has more energy than depression. When I was depressed, I didn't feel like doing anything. I was exhausted all the time. But when I was angry, I felt energized and able to take action, even though it might have been vengeful.

In using the Emotional Scale, you have to move up the chart progressively. You cannot jump from Level 1 (depression) to Level 10 (joy). You need to move up the chart level by level and acknowledge each feeling. In other words, I needed to acknowledge my anger to move up to joy.

The day I wrote down how betrayed I felt, my anger wasn't expressed fully. I needed a safe place to display my rage without being judged. My inner volcano needed to erupt without hurting anyone in the process.

So I waited for a day when no one was home.

One evening, before my elder brother left to meet his friends, he asked if I was okay with staying home alone. He has been very kind since he learned about my depression. He checks in with me regularly and intercepts conversations about money initiated by our parents. But on this particular day, I was secretly waiting for him to leave the house so I could release my pent-up anger...freely.

When he finally left, I immediately went into my room and shut the door. Coincidentally, at this time, I was listening to Stark Sands' *"Soul of a Man"* from the Kinky Boots broadway musical. This song was sung when Charlie, the main character in the show, was at his lowest point in life. He had failed to keep his late father's shoe business alive. This song really got me into the mood for releasing my anger, and I wasn't sure when I would be strong enough again.

I'll never be the soul of a man, noble and wise

Like the soul of a man who lifted me high

Soul of a man, heroic and true

Like the soul of a man that I looked up to

What else could I do?

– Stark Sands

I looped the track and turned the volume up loud so no one could hear me cry and shout. Then, for the next fifteen minutes, I just cried as much as I wanted and shouted as loud as I could. I kept punching my bed with my bare hands until all my betrayal, anger, and hatred were felt and released.

I hated Jason for betraying my trust and disregarding my feelings. Why did he say he wanted to hire me when he couldn't? Why did he give me hope and then take it away? I hated the world for not giving me a chance to prove myself. I could do so much for my company, why wouldn't they trust and hire me? I hated myself for being naive and reckless. I should have listened to my gut feelings and made a better decision. Most of all, I hated the depression that kept coming back to torment me.

"Go away! Go away! Stop making me cry! Stop coming back. I'm sick and tired of you. I don't need you anymore," I shouted to the empty room.

Even though anger is considered negative and undesirable by most people, I needed to express it fully. To let go of a feeling takes away its power over you, but it must first be welcomed and acknowledged. I had tried to let go of anger previously, but it didn't work. Empathy didn't welcome it. She told me it wasn't right to be angry with others, and because my anger wasn't acknowledged I couldn't let it go.

When we are unable to let go of a feeling, we have two options: suppression or expression. I had been suppressing my anger for a long time, which did nothing except keep me mired in depression. In fact, I had reached the point where I was so tired of depression that I would have done anything to get rid of it—even if it required me to get angry. So I let Anger sit in the driving seat for a while and express himself the best he could.

After crying and releasing all my pain, I felt so good. Seventy-five percent of my depression was gone, and I was able to sleep through the night. I had more energy to take action, and I even wrote a few blog posts about depression.

I was finally on track to getting my life back and being productive again.

Chapter 12

Reconciling Anger and Empathy

After being ignored for more than a month, Jason finally called. He must have sensed that I wasn't feeling very friendly towards him, because in my messages I gave short replies like "okay." I also told him not to keep changing the dates for the lessons because it wasn't good for the reputation of his company (yes, I was pissed, but I tried to say it as elegantly as possible). For the most part, I was disenchanted. Whenever he said he wanted to meet, I knew it wouldn't actually happen so there was no need to leave a lengthy reply.

When Jason called, I knew he had read my blog posts about depression. He sounded apologetic, yet defensive. He spent the next hour explaining how sorry he was and what he was going through. He said I should be more open with him and express any issues I had with him directly. He also told me I shouldn't overanalyze the situation on my own.

I had mixed feelings, too. A part of me was angry because he had misunderstood what I'd written. He thought I hadn't considered his feelings. But, in reality, I already understood his behavior. Another part of me felt bad that he was affected by what I had written. I wasn't trying to blame him. I was just expressing my experience in words so I would feel better. I wasn't trying to shame him. I didn't even put his name in the blog posts.

I tried telling him my intention in writing blog posts, but he was too emotional to listen to my explanation. What's more, I realized I was getting angry, impatient, and defensive, too! When I realized I was being reactive, Empathy returned and took control. I just listened and let him share what he had to say; otherwise, the conversation might have never ended! Finally, we agreed to meet later in the week to discuss my role in his company.

***

The lifelong battle between Anger and Empathy had to stop. They needed to work *with* each other.

Empathy was useful. She knew how to handle emotional people. She knew when to step back and listen.

She understood that if I fought with a defensive person, it would just make the situation worse and result in an unnecessary argument. Instead, she used kindness to dissolve any attacks coming my way.

Although Empathy had been good to other people, she was not all that empathetic towards me. There was nothing wrong with taking care of everyone else's feelings, but I was part of "everyone," too. My feelings were also important. Empathy had prevented me from feeling some of my emotions, which caused the episode with depression.

Of course, I understood Jason was having a hard time, and I trusted him when he said he wanted me to join his company. But I couldn't help but feel betrayed and angry towards him every time I thought about how he had behaved towards me when I returned from Bali to work for him. How could I be compassionate and be angry at him at the same time?

One of these feelings must be a lie.

When I first received Jason's reply, I pretended everything was fine and told my family I was alright because I didn't want to feel angry. Anger conflicted with my self-identity. I thought of myself as empathetic and kind, and I believed that by practicing compassion I would be able to defuse my anger. I was wrong. My compassion wasn't authentic to begin with, and I was so hurt by Jason that there wasn't any room for compassion.

In such cases, Empathy should have let Anger take over. Anger knew how to handle these situations better. Contrary to what Empathy thought, Anger wasn't trying to inflict harm on Jason. He was just trying to protect me from injustice and harm. When I wasn't able to express my anger to others, all the blame and pain were directed towards myself. My negative emotions slowly chipped away at my self-worth and caused me to be severely depressed. Every time I tried to get out of depression, I couldn't, because I hadn't given myself permission to be angry. In fact, after this second episode, I realized how Anger had unintentionally helped me resolve my first depression.

All emotions are useful, and this includes anger.

When I told my parents my auditor job was killing my soul, they just told me to suck it up and bear it. At that time, I was infuriated with their response. I kept thinking: *How could they not care about their child? Here I am telling them how I feel, and they ask me to simply bear the pain. Even if they want me to stay in the job, I'm not staying!*

It actually turned out to be the best thing ever, because suddenly I had the energy to look for another job. Later, when I saw my female colleague crying, I became empowered to help myself. There was no way I was going to let anything bully me, including a job. So in the end, I became so brave that I was able to leave my job without another one to replace it, and things just got better.

Anger was my savior. He prevented me from going in a downward spiral. Who knew what would have happened if Anger hadn't stepped in and given me a push in the right direction?

Blocking our feelings and pretending they aren't there doesn't mean they don't exist.

Anger, like other emotions, will find a way to manifest if it is not recognized and released. People who don't get angry can become passive-aggressive. Some might numb their anger with addictions such as food, alcohol, sex, shopping, and entertainment. Some people end up depressed. So expressing anger is vital to emotional stability.

However, even though expressing it fully is healthy, getting stuck in anger isn't. Remaining angry for too long turns us into victims. Whenever something we don't like occurs, we look for someone else to blame and direct our anger towards them. In the long run, we give away our responsibility and power when we rely on external factors and other people to make us happy—and then there are the health issues that come with anger, including heart disease and stroke.

Anger is simply a passageway to the next emotion. When we deny our anger and suppress it, we also deny ourselves feelings of joy, love, and peace. After I released my anger towards Jason, I became more willing to listen to what he had to say. I was no longer controlled by circumstances and found peace through acceptance.

There is a time for anger and a time for empathy. Use anger constructively—its purpose is to protect, not harm—and practice compassion only when it's authentic.

Chapter 13

Seeking Approval

If there is one thing I gained from depression and all the crying, it's clarity. It's as though my tears washed away all the illusions that had been covering my eyes for the past year. I no longer needed to be in the animation industry; it's not how I wanted to spend my life, and I had to accept it and let go of my shame.

I was meant to be a writer.

Jason always complimented me and talked about my talent. All I needed was to figure out what I wanted to focus on. We spent hours discussing what I could do for his company. But my problem wasn't due to a lack of ideas or self-awareness. I knew what I wanted to be intuitively. The problem was: *Will I listen to my own intuition?*

After completing my animation studies, I could have immediately found an animator job, but I didn't. Instead, I felt compelled to complete my book, *Fearless Passion*. Wasn't this an obvious sign of my priorities?

When I was a teen, I had low self-esteem and didn't have many friends. I wrote to cheer myself up. In school, I wrote Chinese essays and represented my class in competitions. At home, I wrote Chinese lyrics and even received an award for Best Lyrics in a songwriting competition. Writing has always been my best friend, supporting me when I've felt lonely. My intuition tried so hard to tell me writing was my best medium, but I doubted it.

Despite the obvious clues, my mind was skeptical. It kept telling me it didn't make sense to be a full-time writer in Singapore. I couldn't find any successful self-published authors in Singapore to learn from, and the reader base in Singapore is small. Self-publishing on Amazon is also difficult for Singaporeans. There isn't any income tax treaty between Singapore and the United States, so Amazon withheld 30 percent of the royalties I earned from the sale of my books. Moreover, I didn't even earn enough from my first book to cash out my royalties. What made me think I could survive as a writer in Singapore? It just didn't make any sense to try and earn a living as a writer.

Even though I had written a book about overcoming fear, I was still afraid to listen to my own intuition. Throughout my period of turmoil, I kept consulting others about business and employment decisions, because I didn't trust myself and I was afraid of failure. I let other people decide my path, because if what other people suggested failed I wouldn't have to take responsibility. It was their ideas that were bad. Every time I asked someone else for an opinion, I was just seeking approval. I was waiting for others to give me their blessings to be a writer.

But the more ideas people offered, the more lost I became, because no one knew how much it meant to me be a writer—only I knew. Rather than claiming the power I already possessed within me, I kept seeking answers from outside of myself.

After my depression episode, everything seemed much clearer. The biggest approval I needed was actually from myself. I no longer had to wait for my parents, brothers, friends, and authority figures to approve of what I did. I didn't even need my mind to give me the green light anymore.

I decided to let my soul do what it was meant to do and allow its true beauty to shine.

With this newfound clarity towards my life and my work, I was determined to tell Jason I wouldn't be joining his company.

I now had the power to make my own decisions to approve or disapprove of whatever was before me.

***

The day came when I was supposed to meet Jason. Right before we started our discussion, I used my newfound courage to tell him straight up about my decision to reject any offer of employment with his company. I could have told him on the phone, but I thought it would be better to resolve any conflict and explain my point of view face-to-face. But little did I know Jason was having similar thoughts.

He breathed a sigh of relief and told me that he didn't want to hire me, but he didn't know how to put it in a nice manner that wouldn't hurt me. He was afraid I was too weak to handle the rejection. His business was in need of people who had a sales and business development background. I didn't have the skills he was looking for, and because of my recent episode of depression he realized I couldn't handle changes well.

Jason had taken a long time to find a perfect opportunity to reject me, but what I really needed from him from the beginning was a definite answer—yes or no. As it was, his behavior had given me false hope and caused needless suffering. Nonetheless, I was glad we had closure so I could finally move on with my life. But something he'd said during the conversation continued to bother me—Jason had referred to me as "weak."

Chapter 14

Men Should Be Allowed to Cry

When Jason said I was weak, I knew he was referring to my inability to handle changes and emotions. So I wasn't completely offended, although I had a different perspective.

I would never consider a depressed person to be weak. Depression is like any other illness or accident. Should someone who's had the flu or cancer be considered weak? Should someone who's been in a car accident be considered weak?

There are some things in life we can't control, and the more we try to control what we can't control, the more we are doomed to suffer.

In fact, depressed people should be considered

strong. I was depressed for two months, and I knew how painful it was, I couldn't imagine the lives of people who had suffered from depression for years. To survive and live through it every day was a real display of courage and strength.

After I wrote three blog posts on depression, things became quite interesting. Friends who read the posts weren't sure if they wanted to talk to me about it. Every time, I mentioned the word "depression," people would cringe and attempt to avoid the topic. One of my friends was brave enough to approach the subject but, even so, he said, "I thought you were sensible. You were always positive. *Why did you let yourself become so depressed?*"

I didn't blame my friends for avoiding and not understanding depression. It was uncomfortable to talk about, and people who have never experienced depression don't know what a depressed person has to go through.

Even for me, I felt uneasy telling others I had depression. I had to think twice before publishing my posts online, especially because I am a man. Men are taught to be strong and confident. We are taught to be emotionally stable. We aren't allowed to cry, especially in public, because crying is a sign of weakness.

If I share my personal experience online, won't everyone

know that I cried (in public)?

However, later I asked myself, *So what if everyone knows I cried in public? Does it even matter?* Sharing or not sharing my experience wouldn't change the fact that I was depressed and cried. Not sharing my experience actually allowed my shame to grow stronger and make my positive sense of self get weaker—and I didn't need other people's perceptions of me to feel weak. I was at my weakest when I hid my feelings and pretended everything was just fine.

So I published my posts. *No more hiding this time round. This time, I would be strong.*

***

On my way to recovery, I began to notice other people who had depression, too—they were celebrities, YouTube stars, bloggers, and normal people like me. I wanted to applaud these people for being brave and sharing their experiences openly. They encouraged me to share my experience, and they also provided valuable information about depression for everyone.

There were two men in particular whose experience I connected with when I watched them on TV. Even though there wasn't any mention of depression, it was easy to empathize with their situations, and I learned a lot about my own feelings through their experiences. It was absolutely strong and courageous of them as men to display their true emotions in public—even though they didn't originally intend to.

Stephen Fishbach (from *Survivor: Cambodia*)

I'm a big fan of the American reality TV show *Survivor*, and I wasn't going to miss it, even when I had depression. Watching *Survivor* was really good, because it distracted me for a while from my troubles. I was so focused on the castaways and the game that I wasn't focusing much on my depression. It was only when one of the contestants, Stephen Fishbach, started crying during his confessions that it reminded me of my own situation.

Stephen had a breakdown when the monsoon rain hit their camp and lasted for days. In his confession, he cried, "I'm scared my body is breaking down. I need some ray of hope. I just need the sun to come out for 15 minutes. I'm not quitting. I'm not quitting. There's no way I'm quitting."

Living in Singapore, I knew how bad the monsoon rain in Southeast Asia can be. Sometimes, there are days of heavy downfall without any relief. Living under a simple shelter, I could imagine how cold and miserable the *Survivor* participants were, and how little they slept at night. This particular season of *Survivor* was different. The theme was *second chances*. It was the first time the contestants were voted in by the viewers to play again. Therefore, all of them felt pressured to do well in the game. There was no way Stephen was going to quit the game and disappoint his fans.

Although I had not shared the same experience as Stephen, I could relate to how he felt. He described perfectly how hopeless a depressed person feels. Every time depression is triggered, it feels like it will never go away:

We cried like the monsoon rain and we couldn't stop. We lived in fear and anxiety constantly, and we couldn't see any hope for the future. On one hand, we didn't want to die and quit our life. But on the other hand, we were so afraid our system would fail us. With all the crying and intense emotions, we just needed *a* gleam of hope—15 minutes would have been enough. We just needed the depression to stop for a while so we could rest and be at peace.

Roger (from *The Joy Truck 3*)

The Joy Truck is a Singapore variety show that helps families in need to raise funds and improve their lives. At the beginning of each show, the hosts interview the beneficiaries. There was one episode that made a huge impression on me. The beneficiary, Roger, couldn't speak or write properly. As the interview progressed, he couldn't help but break down and cry.

Roger was 46 years old, and he was once a successful financial advisor. He used to be the sole breadwinner for his family. But after he had a stroke in 2010, his life changed drastically. The right side of his body was paralyzed and his speech was affected. Roger's elderly father—whom he had once provided for—now had to take care of him. It was heartbreaking.

I understood how helpless and frustrated Roger felt. He was so successful and had everything he needed, but overnight everything was taken away. He could no longer live his familiar life. His biggest asset as a financial advisor used to be his communication skills, but now he couldn't even express himself properly. He had to rely on his family to tell his story during the interview, and it was frustrating because his family couldn't understand exactly what he wanted to say.

That night, after the episode, I had a vision. I saw a

man being lifted high up in the sky, and then suddenly someone pulled the rug out from under his feet. The man fell from the sky and hit the ground with a great impact. He did not die, but he couldn't get back up. *To rise up so high, only to have the rug pulled out from under you – how devastating is that?*

Depression felt like this. My blindside felt like this. Of course, people might think it's silly to compare my situation with Roger's. I could easily get a job with my skills and qualifications. It wasn't as though I was physically impaired.

I used to think my pain was insignificant, too, so I ignored it. *But I was wrong. Pain is pain,* no matter how big or small we think it is. We shouldn't compare our own pain with others and downplay our experience. The more we act brave when we are suffering, the worst our pain will get.

It wasn't just the pain; it was also the shock. Sudden changes in life such as the death of someone important, being diagnosed a critical illness, or being blindsided can cause a person to become depressed. I believed Jason would hire me, no matter what, because he was so enthusiastic. Then, when he didn't, I couldn't see a way out of the situation because I was in shock and unable able to process the reality of what had happened.

At times like this, shouldn't we be allowed to cry?

***

It's easy to share our achievements, using obstacles to prove how much we have overcome. It's also easier to be strong and proud than it is to be weak and ashamed.

But what if our personal experience could help others and let them know they aren't alone? What if our stories could inspire another depressed person to seek help and recover? Most importantly, what if society allowed men to cry and embrace their real feelings—could it have saved those who committed suicide?

Life isn't about being strong or *pretending* we are strong to impress others. It takes courage to be authentic with our feelings and acknowledge that real strength comes from recognizing our moments of weakness.

After I shared my depression online, everyone knew about my shame and low self-esteem. But I was the strongest I had ever been in my life.

Chapter 15

Relapse and Lessons Learned

After I released my anger, I felt better. I was healing from depression slowly and forgiving Jason. I returned to my writing schedule in the morning. I also applied for jobs to help fund the books I wanted to write.

But still, I felt unsettled. It was as though there was 25 percent of depression floating around within me that didn't want to go away, and I didn't know why. Perhaps it was because I was having trouble finding a job that felt right and I was getting anxious. I wasn't moving anywhere in life and I felt stuck. I became easily agitated over the slightest things.

At one point, I couldn't tolerate being in the same room with my younger brother. I had to get out of the house and walk around the neighborhood. As I was listening to a self-help audio, I reached a platform at the edge of the river and a scary thought came to me, *Jump down and everything will be resolved.*

I stood there frozen, staring at the river, not knowing what to do. If I jumped down, I would definitely die. I didn't know how to swim and there was no one nearby to rescue me. I realized that after a month of relative stability my suicidal impulse had come back again. I shook my head, trying to get rid of the voice in my head.

Don't believe the voice. You're fine, I told myself as I walked away from the river.

When I reached the next platform, another voice spoke, *I know you're suffering. Jump down and you will find peace.*

This time, the river looked more alluring than before. It looked beautiful, peaceful, and still — which was just what I needed right now. I contemplated the situation. I couldn't even hear the audio playing in the background. My mind was totally focused on whether to jump or not. I was tempted to *become one with the river.* But luckily, after a few minutes, I awoke from my deep thought and regained consciousness of my physical surroundings.

I didn't dare to walk outside anymore. It was so terrifying to hear suicidal voices in my head again. I sat down on a bench near the river in disbelief that I nearly jumped off the platform. It seemed like there was nothing I could do to get rid of the voices. All I could do was to sit there and do nothing.

But as I continued to sit and let time pass, everything slowed down. For the first time, I saw how beautiful my neighborhood had become over the past year. The bench I was sitting on wasn't here before. There wasn't any shade or resting area a year ago. Vibrant red flowers had been planted on the vegetated swales along the river, and the platform I had stood on was meant to be a lookout deck for people to enjoy the scenery—not to commit suicide!

The magnificent surroundings allowed me to feel calm and present. In that moment, I had no worries or pain, just deep appreciation for being alive. I got up and walked back to one of the platforms. As I looked at the river, the thought of jumping down crossed my mind again.

However, this time, another voice inside of me spoke, saying: *I don't want to die. I want to live. I didn't survive childhood epilepsy so I could die now. I was given a chance to live until this day for a purpose. Be in touch with that purpose.*

This voice was so loud and firm that it drowned out all the uneasiness I was experiencing inside.

That day, I knew I was completely healed from depression. I had passed the test when I chose life over death. I realized I didn't want to die; I just wanted the pain to end. Once I welcomed the pain instead of running away from it, everything including the pain itself dissolved. Pain is like a car spinning out of control; eventually, it will come to a stop. Panicking doesn't help. It only makes the car spin even more out of control. The suicidal thoughts I experienced were just trying to protect me from my feelings. They were not meant to kill me.

When I surrendered to the beauty around me, everything was perfect. Humans naturally know how to survive if we allow things to simply *be* and not resist.

The best way to end suffering is to accept what is and surrender.

There are meaningful lessons to be learned from each experience. So, what was I supposed to learn from depression? What if depression wasn't here to cause pain and suffering? What if it was here to teach me something? What would the lesson be?

I believe I became depressed a second time in order to write about depression. The universe didn't want me to die; the intention was to help me learn and grow. I was given the opportunity to experience depression again so I could understand how depressed people feel, and then do something to help lift them up. The universe wanted me to share my insights with others who need to hear the message, especially those who are highly sensitive. We are never given challenges in life we can't handle. Every challenge is meant to teach us something.

I was thankful for my experience. Here are the three main things I learned:

Lesson #1 - Trust My Intuition

I never dared to be a full-time writer until after I had depression. Whenever I deviated from what I was meant to be, depression came to guide me back to the right path— the first time, when I felt trapped as an auditor, and the second time when I felt lost in the animation industry.

Depression was my career path compass.

It might seem absurd to let depression be my guide, but it happened that way because I didn't listen to hints from my intuition. I either didn't trust the hints or I didn't take action. The universe had no choice but to use depression to wake me up from my unconsciousness. If I had faith in my intuition, I would not have needed depression.

Sometimes, I couldn't differentiate between the voice of intuition and the voice of fear. Now, I know *intuition is the persistent voice.* Fear fades away eventually; intuition sticks around. My depression went away only because I learned the message it was here to teach. Intuition comes from a place of love. It understands what we love the most and points out the truth. Fear, on the other hand, causes resistance and makes us feel trapped.

Now I'm a writer, and I no longer need to seek a full-time job for security. I earn just enough from odd jobs to meet my basic needs and fund my books, while learning to grow my self-publishing business.

I continue to try and trust my intuition and do my best to be a full-time writer.

Lesson #2 - Love Myself Fully

Depression also made me realize I didn't love myself completely. My self-esteem had improved tremendously over the years, but my self-worth was attached to what I had, what I did, and what I achieved. *My love for myself was conditional.* When I didn't have a job, my self-love disappeared. In fact, something was lurking in the background, waiting for an opportunity to pry open my past wounds and break me apart. I also realized that I agreed to help Jason because his praise made me feel worthy.

High self-esteem is not something that can be built overnight. It's a repetitive process of changing unworthiness to worthiness. After my depression came back, I listened to the self-help audio I had been neglecting for the past year; I also read new books on self-esteem. I even created a self-love project for 2016 on my blog to remind myself and others to love themselves.

Daily love and care for myself doesn't mean I won't feel depressed again. But seven years of self-help knowledge did allow me to become more aware and recover from depression quicker.

Most people only seek help when they have a problem, but taking care of yourself every day is important. Depression isn't something we can be done with after we overcome it. It's critical to build a strong foundation we can rely on in times of need.

Lesson #3 - Embrace All Feelings

As a highly sensitive person, I tend to be overwhelmed by other people's emotions. My experience of depression reminded me to be more in tune with my own feelings. All emotions have a purpose. They are neither good nor bad. They are just energy that will go away, eventually. It takes courage to be vulnerable and acknowledge feelings such as shame. But the more we welcome our feelings and express them, the easier it is to let them go.

Before depression, I never realized I had a problem with anger. I felt bad every time I expressed it, but I didn't realize I had so much resistance to it. Now I understand I can be angry without being destructive. Anger is just trying to protect me from self-inflicted harm.

I also learned the difference between *knowing* and *believing* something to be true. Jason didn't intend to blindside me, but that didn't mean I didn't feel betrayed and hurt. Hurt is hurt, no matter whether it is intentional or not. I should have embraced my feelings and not justified them. Only when I addressed my feelings was I able to move on and forgive.

In the end, my circumstances didn't change—all that changed were my feelings about the circumstances.

***

Even though I didn't jump into the river, I did die that day — the old me was dead and a new spiritual me was born. I felt calmer and more at peace. I started reading spiritual books such as *The Shift* by Dr. Wayne Dyer, *The Power of Now* by Eckhart Tolle, and *I Am* by Howard Falco. These are books I wouldn't have understood before I had depression.

So...perhaps my trip to Bali wasn't meant to be entrepreneurial, but rather a spiritual quest. I learned more about myself in Bali than what to do for my business. All my plans were thrown out of the window as I began to discover who I am as a person.

I had signed up for a lot of courses, but *the biggest teacher is life*. Perhaps we need to die multiple times in order to realize the true meaning of life.

I'm grateful I died that day.

Want to Know More?

You can learn more about loving yourself and being a highly sensitive introvert on my blog, www.nerdycreator.com.

I have dedicated this year to self-love and I'm writing more books and posts on this topic.

If you want instant updates on my latest books and offers, please subscribe to my email list below. I run special promotions and offer free or discounted books on Amazon regularly.

Sign up now at: http://www.nerdycreator.com/discount/

Did You Like *The Emotional Gift?*

Thank you for purchasing my book and spending time to read it.

Before you go, I'd like to ask you for a small favor. Could you please take a couple of minutes to leave a review for this book on Amazon?

Your feedback will not only help me grow as an author, it will also help those who need the message in this book. So, thank you!

Please leave a review at:

http://www.nerdycreator.com/the-emotional-gift/

Resources

Fearless Passion: Find the Courage to Do What You Love, by Yong Kang Chan; 2014; Yong Kang Chan; Singapore, Singapore
For more books by the author, please go to www.nerdycreator.com/books.

The Sedona Method: Your Key to Lasting Happiness, Success, Peace, and Emotional Well-being by Hale Dwoskin with a Foreword by Jack Canfield; 2015; Sedona Press, Sedona, Arizona

Effortless Success: Living the Law of Attraction (Audio CD) by Jack Canfield and Paul Scheele; 2008; Learning Strategies Corporation, Minnetonka, Minnesota

Dr. Brené Brown's Ted talk entitled *Listening to Shame.*

The Gifts of Imperfection: Let Go of Who You Think You're Supposed to be and Embrace Who You Are by Dr. Brené Brown, 2010, Hazelden, Center City, Minnesota

The Shift: Taking Your Life from Ambition to Meaning by Dr. Wayne Dyer; 2010; Hay House, Carlsbad, California

The Power of Now: A Guide to Spiritual Enlightenment by Eckhart Tolle; 2004; Namaste Publishing, Vancouver, BC, Canada

I Am: The Power of Discovering Who You Really Are by Howard Falco; 2010; TarcherPerigee, New York, New York

About the Author

Yong Kang Chan, best known as Nerdy Creator, is a writer, author and storyteller. Having low self-esteem growing up, he cares about topics such as personal growth, self-love, spirituality and passion. He believes stories can make the world a better place and he writes to lift people up.

Apart from writing posts to help people with low self-esteem, he shares insights on being an introvert and a highly sensitive person (HSP) on his blog, www.nerdycreator.com.

Based in Singapore, Yong Kang is also a regular contributor on Lifehack and his blog post on introverts has over 27,000 shares.

CPSIA information can be obtained
at www.ICGtesting.com
Printed in the USA
LVOW13s1432280817
546675LV00032B/1741/P